An Interrupted Conversation

by

Phil Houseal

Acknowledgments

Thanks to the Dick Culbertson family
for allowing me to share the wit of their father, husband,
grandfather, and hero with the world.

Thanks to The Texas Community Education Association,
the organization through which I first met and later worked with
Dick and many other fine people supporting lifelong learning.

Special Thanks Sherman D. Durst, who first suggested this
column would make a worthy book. Sherman passed away from
his own health battles in 2013.

And Thanks to all of you readers,
who are going to help finish this story.

About the Author

Phil Houseal is a writer,
educator, musician, and owner of
Full House PR, a public relations firm
that tells the story of your product, service, or business.

www.fullhouseproductions.net
phil@fullhouseproductions.net

Also by Phil Houseal

Finding Fredericksburg:
A Self-Guided Tour through Historic Fredericksburg, Texas
www.findingfredericksburg.com

Playing To A Full House:
The People Who Make the Music of the Texas Hill Country
www.fullhouseproductions.net

Sam Has Ants
A delightful story for children ages 3 to 7
www.samhasants.com

Also available on Amazon.com
amazon.com/author/philhouseal

Introduction

I first met Dick Culbertson around 1995. Or rather, he tackled me. I had just finished a breakout session at a conference for our Texas Community Education Association in Austin. I was walking down the hall when I felt a strong grip grab my elbow from behind.

"Hey, young man, we need to talk."

I turned and had my first glimpse of Dick Culbertson. Even then he was into his 70s, and though slightly stooped and white haired, his jutting jaw and clear eyes betrayed the man's earnestness and energy. He steered me to a chair and we had the first of many intense conversations that went on for 15 years.

Dick believed passionately in the value of lifelong learning.

During his career in the Air Force, flying fighters in Korea and Vietnam, he helped establish the Community College of the Air Force. After retiring to San Antonio, he continued his active volunteer career on behalf of the Texas Community Education Association, serving on or helping form citizen advisory councils for local, state, and national associations.

Mayors, senators, governors, and future presidents opened doors to Dick.

Dick worked the phones constantly. He called me up regularly and in his gruff way nudged, cajoled, and pushed me on to be a better follower, and then become a better leader as I went on to serve on the state and national associations.

He never minced words. And he never failed to make an impression on me. After every phone call I started writing down comments he said, loving the colorful way he had with words, and appreciating the wisdom lying beneath.

When Dick was well into his 80s, I asked him to give me his 100 truths–100 bits of wisdom to pass along to help the rest of us navigate the world he was looking back on.

To my surprise and joy, he wrote them out in longhand on a yellow legal pad and sent them to me.

Some are simple. Some are repetitive. Some are a little hard to understand. But all are real. All are pure Dick Culbertson. With this book, I can share a little bit of him with more people.

Here they are...

1

We learn only by looking back.

2

It's easy to be humble if you
are a great leader.

3

Please don't ask me "why?" before you do it. By the time I explain it to you I could have done it myself.

4

Appreciate your parents. If they knew what a self-centered, self-aggrandizing little bastard you would turn out to be they still would have had you.

5

If you start it, finish it.

6

Judging others is a dangerous game.

7

Communicate, communicate, communicate.

8

Honor our great men and women before they're dead.

9

**A great companion is
the finest thing in the world.**

10

She anticipates my needs
before I ever get the thoughts
out of my mind.

11

Human pettiness isn't
worth recognizing.
It rots in its own uselessness.

12

Your actions speak so loud I can't hear what you are saying.

13

My mother
will always be the wisest person
I have ever known.

14

Wisdom was hard to come by:
don't sell it cheap.

15

Ideas, ideas, ideas...
how great thou art.

16

I never met a woman that wasn't smarter than me.

17

Freedom isn't only the best thing; it's the only thing.

18

Our minds drive everything we do.

19

You are a human becoming,
one way or another.

20

A straight line is not always
the best way to get there.

21

**Wishing is great.
Now make it happen.**

22

A storm cannot often be controlled. The secret of survival is riding it out.

23

Success is in the minds of others.

24

It's a long, long road to
Tipperary;
enjoy each inch of it.

25

Where your attention is,
is where you are.

26

Your brain is what
you tell it to do.

27

I never have had to ask you
if you love me.

28

Just being together and
doing nothing is the
test of happiness.

29

In this world of ours,
it is every nation for itself.

30

Learners are scarce.
Just look around you.

31

Truthfulness must be administered carefully.

32

A sincere smile disarms.

33

I respect you unless
you prove otherwise.

34

Genius is rare: cultivate it.

35

Prosperity is not having to worry about money to make ends meet.

36

Liberty is about
freedom of movement.

37

To hope is great, but it must be covered by action.

38

Each day is opportunity.
Use it.

39

Impossible is only a word.

40

Each life is precious.
Especially your own.

41

Fly right and there is
no worrying.

42

If you go up, stay there.

43

Own a piece of land and
your country is yours.

44

Wish me not a long life,
but a healthy one.

45

Integrity isn't acquired -
it's in you or not.

46

Good friends
make great companions.

47

Fool me once, and it's over.

48

An intellectual thief is the worst kind.

49

The fastest thing in the world
is time.

50

Good, clean humor
is prideless.

51

Lovers are forever.

52

Keeping your word is easy if you meant it originally.

53

You are known for what you do.

54

Management is leading.

55

One who follows intelligently
may someday lead.

56

A thing of beauty keep.

57

Your view of virtue defines it.

58

Always consider options and alternatives.

59

Coordinate, coordinate, coordinate.

60

I never say never
because I might do it.

61

Simple is as simple does.

62

Find your interest and find success.

63

Identify your talent and develop it.

64

Music is life's pacifier.

65

A swift kick must be
placed right.

66

Duplicity is ultimately
self-revealing.

67

An ounce of loyalty is worth
100 pounds of B.S.

68

The people you think you fool
will make one of you.

69

Flowers brighten the home
and the heart.

70

Beauty is in the heart.

71

Giving without obligation
is the only kind.

72

If you think you are a leader,
just turn around.

73

Humor never harms.

74

The brain has endless elasticity
for creativity.

75

When action accompanies
mind work, it happens.

76

If it's right, you or no one else
is hurt by it.

77

Meanness means loneliness.

78

Moderation equates
to longevity.

79

Growing old gracefully means accepting reality.

80

Treat yourself to some decent experience each day.

81

What is shared is kept.

82

It takes a long time to wise up.

83

We came here to learn;
please keep us awake.

84

We never run out of time;
we just mismanage it.

85

Stay around
the brightest and
most successful
where possible.

86

Money can show appreciation
without obligation.

87

Habits are who you are.

88

A simmering pot
will not explode.

89

Your main concern is good health.

90

A trend in anything needs to
be understood.

91

Learning is two-fold:

Formal (schools),
and Informal (experience).

Credential as much of it
as possible.

92

Wisdom is your profit from
understanding experiences.

93

Piss off all but six people; then make them your pallbearers.

Dick's list stopped at 93...

...seven short of 100.

A few months after his messages stopped arriving, I found out my friend Dick was in an extended care facility in another state.

One day I wrote him that I still had lessons to learn from him, and asked for seven more "truths" of life so we could reach 100. His daughter-in-law replied with the news Dick had died at 4:40 that very morning.

She wrote that Dick could no longer speak the previous few days, but my request had made him cry.

Every year we lose many friends and relatives. Often the ones that affect us most deeply are the people who are not necessarily pillars of society. In fact, some of the more interesting are "rounders"–they scheme, finagle, infuriate, and are always keep you off balance. But deep inside is an unassailable soul of goodness. It's as if they know life is a game and they are playing it with gusto. The spark they leave is that they seem to be the people who are more alive than the rest of us.

After they are gone, well-meaning survivors try to console you with phrases such as "they are in a better place" and "they will always be with you."

I don't buy that.

I miss them.

Like an interrupted conversation.

Complete the conversation.

Write in your seven best pieces of advice or lessons learned so far in your life. Then keep them to refer back to, or pass this book along to someone in your life who can benefit from it.

Go to the next pages and fill in your best pieces of advice.

95

96

97

98

99

100

Thank you.

If you discover that seven truths are not enough, write more.
Maybe even write your own book.

For your family.

For your friends.

For yourself.

Dick Culbertson–1916-2005

Dick and Betty Culbertson at a dinner in his honor.

Dick was proud of his flying days.

Culbertson   02/06/2005
Richard Nixon Culbertson, Sr. LtCol, USAF (Ret) Nov 24, 1916 Feb 3, 2005 Dick passed away
last Thursday morning after a lengthy battle with ALS. A Command Pilot, he had a full
career in the United States Air Force, retiring in 1976 while stationed at Randolph AFB.
After retiring he worked for the Texas Department of Human Services and became an active
leader in the Texas Community Education Association at the local, state and national
level. He was also a past president of the Senior Citizens Council of Bexar County, and
stayed very active in the San Antonio volunteer community. Dick and Betty moved to Tucson,
AZ in November of 2003 after 32 years in San Antonio. He is survived by his wife of 63
years, Betty, his four sons; Rick, Ron, Gary and David Culbertson and their wives, 8
grandchildren and 4 great-grandchildren. Only when you drink from the river of silence
shall you indeed sing. And when you have reached the mountain top, then you shall begin to
climb. And when the earth shall claim your limbs then shall you truly dance. (Kahlil
Gibran) A memorial service is planned at 11:00 AM at Broadway Proper, 400 S. Broadway
Place, Tucson, AZ. Betty asks that in lieu of flowers donations be sent to: The Texas
Community Education Foundation, 1121 Second Street, Kerrville, TX 78028.

Dick liked to play harmonica, and loved to present–and receive–awards.

*Dick could open doors, convincing Governors and Senators to sign
proclamations in support of community education.*

Community Education is
the process by which the citizens in a school district,
using the resources and facilities of the district,
organize to support each other and to solve
their mutual education problems
and meet their mutual lifelong needs.

To learn more
www.tcea.com

www.fullhouseproductions.net

www.ingramcontent.com/pod-product-compliance
Lightning Source LLC
Chambersburg PA
CBHW060947040426
42445CB00011B/1044